Contents

Introduction...1

Motivation..1

Outline..2

Scope..2

Funding..3

US Federal Research..4

Industry Research..4

Test Facilities..4

Inventory of Research Projects on Oil Spills in Arctic Waters.................................5

Prior Research Provides a Foundation...6

Funding of Oil Spill Research..7

FEDERAL ARCTIC MARINE OIL SPILL RESEARCH EFFORTS..9

Department of the Interior | MMS, BOEMRE, ONRR, BOEM, BSEE, USGS...............................9

Department of Commerce | NOAA...12

Department of Defense | USACE, USN..13

Department of Homeland Security | USCG..14

Other Federal Agencies...15

COORDINATION OF FEDERAL R&D EFFORTS...16

OTHER ARCTIC MARINE OIL SPILL R&D EFFORTS...18

Nonprofit Organizations..18

Industry (US and Non-US)...19

Canada...22

Private Consultants..24

Other Current Activities of Interest and Published R&D Plans..................................25

USARC RECOMMENDATIONS...28

Spill Delineation and Mitigation, Including Containment and Countermeasures...................28

Oil Spill Response Technologies for Cleanup and Recovery of Oil...............................29

Data Management Tools Currently Being Developed, and the Fate of Oil
    and Its Effects on the Environment...29

General..30

Introduction

This "white paper" is a compilation of research on oil spills in ice-covered Arctic waters and recommendations for future work. We identify research entities in governmental, nongovernmental, industrial, and private organizations, and provide an inventory of research projects. Given that much work is currently in progress, we provide only a snapshot in time, and an introduction to the topic.

While an in-depth evaluation of the research results, a prioritization of research and development gaps, and a critical examination of the connection between research and oil spill response capability are undoubtedly important topics, they are beyond the scope of this effort. We hope that our foray into this subject encourages others to address these critical topics. Finally, the US Arctic Research Commission (USARC) closes this paper with recommendations for additional research on the topic of oil spills in ice-covered Arctic waters.

Motivation

We wrote this paper for several reasons. First, because interest in oil and gas development in the Arctic is on the rise, as is marine shipping, the likelihood of oil spills is increasing. Climate change, the retreat of Arctic ice, and global economic demand suggest that oil and gas prospects will be explored and eventually developed on the outer continental shelf of Alaska and in remote, icy waters of other Arctic nations. Increased Arctic marine transportation, and greater oil and gas exploration and production, amplify the possibility of oil spills.

Prior exploration and limited development have occurred in this region, but recent spills in other areas, such as the Gulf of Mexico and the North Sea, have heightened awareness and concern regarding the adequacy of spill prevention and cleanup techniques in ice-infested waters, including those characterized by intact sea ice sheets, broken ice conditions, and slushy conditions.

Second, we attempt to address the basic question, "What research is being done to prevent or respond to oil spills in the Arctic?" As it turns out, several entities are engaged in this activity, including domestic and foreign governments (federal and state), industry, nonprofit organizations, and private consultants.

The third reason is timeliness. Royal Dutch Shell has demonstrated a long-term interest in the outer continental shelf of Alaska, and had planned, in summer 2012, substantial Arctic exploratory drilling operations on two lease holdings in the Beaufort and Chukchi Seas. Because of several challenges, including damage to a spill containment dome (aka "capping stack") during a testing accident, Shell decided, on September 17, 2012, to postpone deep (beyond 1400 feet) drilling in the Alaskan Arctic for at least a year.

Fourth, because oil spill preparedness is a nuanced issue, where the biases of supporters and detractors sometimes lead to selective highlighting, which may confuse the public, we try to present here an unbiased inventory of research, as well as some impartial recommendations on the topic.

Some praised Shell's significant preparation efforts and safety plans, but others raised questions about the feasibility of oil spill response in remote regions. Spills in ice-infested waters and deployment of cleanup technologies pose many challenges. Advocates of offshore oil exploration and development in the Arctic point to the shallow-water locations of these low-pressure-formation prospects and the lack of problems during past drilling efforts. Beyond the obvious logistical and infrastructure challenges of Arctic exploration and development, opponents cite the paucity of techniques for effective cleanup of spills in and under ice, and the uncertain fate and transport of oil in the Arctic Ocean. Concerns have also been raised about the likelihood of long-term impacts on the environment, on the subsistence culture of Alaska Natives and other local inhabitants, and about their dependence on a clean and healthy ecosystem.

Given the continuing discussion about oil and gas development in the Arctic, it is important to review and attempt to answer this question, "What research is being done on oil spills in ice-covered waters?"

Outline

The paper begins with a summary of federal efforts in three topic areas: (1) spill demarcation and mitigation, including containment and countermeasures; (2) oil spill response technologies for cleanup and recovery of oil, including affiliated data management tools; and (3) the fate of oil and its effects on the environment.

Following this summary is a discussion of the work of the Interagency Coordinating Committee on Oil Pollution Research (ICCOPR), whose mission is to coordinate oil pollution research among the federal agencies. The third section describes research efforts by other federal and state agencies, universities, and private entities. The final section highlights nonfederal activities of interest, and plans for additional research.

The white paper focuses primarily on research from the last decade, but it also references prior results, back to the 1980s, because current initiatives build largely on that body of work. USARC's recommendations for future research are included at the end of the paper.

Scope

Our task is to develop a list of organizations and entities that are conducting research on oil spills in Arctic waters and an inventory of research projects on that subject. We also provide a brief introduction to the research and the context within which it is conducted.

With regard to scope, we must also be clear as to what is not included in this white paper. Importantly, we stress that a scientific and technological assessment of the quality of the prior research results is beyond USARC's immediate abilities. Determining, in detail, whether research and development projects produced valuable results and measurable advances, or not, is certainly an important task, and one that should be undertaken by qualified researchers.

To this end, we note that the following text from the draft implementation strategy for National Ocean Policy (http://www.whitehouse.gov/sites/default/files/microsites/ceq/

national_ocean_policy_draft_implementation_plan_01-12-12.pdf) assigns such a duty to the US Coast Guard and the Bureau of Ocean Energy Management: "…assessments of current scientific research as well as traditional knowledge related to the impacts of resource development and pollution applicable to the Arctic."

We also chose not to address the connection between research and the capacity to use research results in an actual oil spill response. And we do not assess the adequacy of in-place infrastructure, which is clearly critical to such a response. Although widely recognized as a critical and overarching concern, issues surrounding the regional response and recovery requirements, as well as systems and capacity, are topics we hope will be addressed by knowledgeable experts, perhaps motivated by this paper.

Funding

The allocation of funding for research is a fundamental issue. With respect to government funding for oil spill research, we rely on a report from the US Government Accountability Office (Report GAO-11-319, Federal Oil and Gas, March 2011, http://www.gao.gov/assets/320/317056.pdf) that cited a total cumulative expenditure of $164 million for the 11 years from 2000 to 2010 inclusive. Importantly, we readily acknowledge that some advances in oil spill response science, developed in non-Arctic regions, can certainly be applied to the Arctic.

Nevertheless, this expenditure ($164M) is significantly less than the funding dedicated to advance technology associated with oil exploration and production. It's also significantly less than what the government earns through lease sales. For example, compared to this amount, the 2008 Minerals Management Service (MMS) lease sale in the Chukchi Sea netted $2.7 billion, and Shell Oil is reported to have spent a total of $4.5 billion, thus far, in leasing costs and in preparation to explore their lease holdings in this area and in the Beaufort Sea.

In reviewing the manner in which the federal government funds research, USARC sees a significant shortcoming with respect to support for the National Oceanic and Atmospheric Administration (NOAA). We underscore the fact that NOAA is the only federal agency with oil spill preparedness, response,

and restoration responsibilities under the Oil Pollution Act of 1990 (OPA90) that does not receive a direct appropriation from the Oil Spill Liability Trust Fund (OSLTF) for research and development. USARC strongly recommends that NOAA receive funding from the OSLTF.

Research funding should be provided for both basic research (commonly academic) and applied. While basic research has led to greater understanding, many other improvements in oil spill prevention and response have resulted from actual testing (both in the field and in test facilities), demonstrations and experimental trials, drills, literature and technology reviews, and hands-on application and experience.

Funding should be directed to projects that show the greatest promise for results that will improve spill prevention and response. Basic research should demonstrate excellent intellectual merit, while applied research should also be rigorously vetted and should be performance-based.

In short, USARC calls for greater funding for research to prevent and respond to oil spills in the Arctic. As George Orwell said, "We have now sunk to a depth at which restatement of the obvious is the first duty of intelligent men."

US Federal Research

Arctic oil spill research conducted by the US federal government addresses environmental stewardship, marine transportation, and commercial development of natural resources. A small percentage of the revenue that the US government collects from the oil industry, through the Department of the Interior's (DOI) Office of Natural Resources Revenue (ONRR), is invested in research.

For example, the Bureau of Ocean Energy Management (DOI/BOEM) conducts research on the environmental and economic impact of developing the resource, and the Bureau of Safety and Environmental Enforcement (DOI/BSEE) focuses on oil spill prevention, preparedness, detection, and cleanup. Other examples are described below, and in an online table that accompanies this white paper (http://www.arctic.gov/publications/oil_spills_tableA.pdf). Government-funded research initiatives are primarily solicited via the Broad Agency Announcement (BAA) process, but other mechanisms, including research conducted within agencies, are used as well.

Industry Research

The oil and gas industry also conducts research on oil spill prevention and response in Arctic waters. A recent example is noteworthy. In January 2012, the International Association of Oil & Gas Producers (OGP) announced an Oil Spill Response Technology Joint Industry Program (JIP) focusing on oil spill recovery in ice and spill response in Arctic marine waters. Below, we discuss this JIP in detail.

One of the first tasks of this JIP has been to collect and review the current state of knowledge on the subject. Some of the relevant reports they identified include:

- American Petroleum Institute and the Joint Industry Program on Oil Spill Recovery in Ice, *Spill Response in the Arctic Offshore*, 2012, http://www.api.org/~/media/Files/EHS/Clean_Water/Oil_Spill_Prevention/Spill-Response-in-the-Arctic-Offshore.ashx
- SINTEF, Report no. 32, *Joint Industry Program on Oil Spill Contingency for Arctic and Ice-Covered Waters, Summary Report*, 2010, http://www.sintef.no/project/JIP_Oil_In_Ice/Dokumenter/publications/JIP-rep-no-32-Summary-report.pdf
- Environmental Studies Research Funds, Canada, Report No. 177, *Beaufort Sea Oil Spills State of Knowledge Review and Identification of Key Issues*, 2010, http://www.esrfunds.org/pdf/177.pdf

Test Facilities

US test facilities support research on the fate of oil in ice-covered waters. Two examples are the Ohmsett Facility in Leonardo, New Jersey, and the refrigerated facilities at the US Army Corps of Engineers Cold Region Research and Engineering Laboratory (CRREL) in Hanover, New Hampshire.

Ohmsett provides independent and objective performance testing of full-scale oil spill response equipment and marine renewable energy systems (wave energy conversion devices), and improves technologies through research and development. "OHMSETT" (http://www.ohmsett.com) was originally an acronym for Oil and Hazardous Materials Simulated Environmental Test Tank. As oil is the only hazardous material now tested, the name is now just "Ohmsett," and it is referred to as "The National Oil Spill Response Research & Renewable Energy Test Facility." It is owned by the US Navy, and is maintained and operated by BSEE through a contract with MAR Inc. The facility conducts tests with oil under various simulated sea states.

CRREL, which has expertise in cold regions science and technology, has refrigerated facilities to evaluate oil behavior in and under ice. Tests conducted at CRREL are summarized at http://www.crrel.usace.army.mil/innovations/oil_spill_research. The proximity of the two research facilities enables collaboration on projects, leveraging the expertise of research staff.

Currently, Alaska Clean Seas, a not-for-profit oil spill response cooperative whose membership includes oil and pipeline companies operating on the North Slope of Alaska, is collaborating with CRREL to design an oil and ice testing tank at Prudhoe Bay, Alaska. Two of the design criteria are: nonferrous construction to minimize electromagnetic interference for testing oil detection antennae, and adequate depth to test remotely and autonomously operated vehicles (ROV/AOV).

Importantly, these facilities are critically valuable research facilities because it is currently illegal in the United States to conduct in situ field testing of procedures to respond to oil spills by intentionally spilling oil in the natural environment.

Inventory of Research Projects on Oil Spills in Arctic Waters

An inventory of 203 research projects on oil spills in Arctic waters has been compiled, and are listed in an online table that accompanies this white paper (http://www.arctic.gov/publications/oil_spills_tableA.pdf). The projects, mostly funded by the US government, industry, and Canada, are categorized as follows:

a. Assessments and workshops (18 projects)
b. Fate and behavior of oil (5)
c. Environmental effects (3)
d. Detection, mapping and tracking (33)
e. Mitigation (116)
f. Testing standards (8)
g. Recent field demonstrations (post 2000) (9)
h. Miscellaneous (11)

For each project, we provide a description that includes the subdiscipline of research, relevant website links, a description of the project, the name of the organization that conducted the research, the name of the sponsor, the year of the study, the objective, and the name of the research facility (e.g., Ohmsett), if one was used.

Also online, courtesy of Mr. Larry Dietrick, Director of the Division of Spill Prevention and Response in the State of Alaska's Department of Environmental Conservation, is a table of the 45 project titles and descriptions for initiatives that have been supported by State of Alaska between the years 2000 and 2010 (http://www.arctic.gov/publications/oil_spills_tableB.pdf). Note that these projects include Arctic and non-Arctic initiatives, as well as terrestrial and marine environments.

After consulting a variety of sources, including discussions with partners, reading the peer-reviewed and "gray" literature, tracking requests for proposals, and attending conferences, it is clear that a considerable amount of work has been done, and continues to be, and in a variety of research areas, to understand the behavior and fate of oil in ice-covered waters. This understanding provides a credible foundation for applied research and engineering designs aimed at minimizing the risk of an accident, and, should one occur, developing more effective response and recovery techniques.

The breadth and value of this body of knowledge may be underappreciated by the general public, and if so, greater efforts need to be made to communicate the value of this information to the layperson and to media representatives.

Nonetheless, three significant areas deserve additional research: preparedness, response effectiveness, and damage assessment.

PREPAREDNESS

- Developing oil detection and mapping techniques that are independent of ice conditions, rapidly deployable, and can be quickly interpreted in the field. Accurate assessment of the size and area of the oil spill will dictate the appropriate magnitude of the response effort. Timely assessment will minimize the impacted area. Techniques that need enhancement are satellite and airborne sensors for cursory assessment, and refined delineation via airborne and underwater systems.
- Establishing baseline environmental conditions and assessing environmentally sensitive areas. In studies commissioned by BOEM and by various nongovernmental organizations, much of the Chukchi and Beaufort coasts have been identified as areas of heightened ecological significance. Large swaths of the shoreline zones are typically shallow and composed of ice-rich permafrost soils (though experiencing thawing in many locations). The impacts of crude and dispersed oil deposition on these shorelines and the cleanup techniques available should be assessed.
- Determining the practicality of using robots and ROVs/

AOVs to assist in the cleanup process. Such technology could improve the response effectiveness in severe weather conditions, dark, dirty, or dangerous situations, or in unstable ice conditions.
- Field testing and training of techniques by the responders to assure familiarity with processes before they have to be deployed for a spill.
- Modeling of oil in, under, and within ice-infested waters. Better determination of how oil accumulates, disperses, and degrades (both biologically and nonbiologically).
- Researching options to minimize and/or mitigate the risk associated with vessel use and carriage of heavy-grade fuel oil in the Arctic.
- Compiling and integrating the datasets necessary for Arctic oil spill planning, coordination, and response that would be used in NOAA's Arctic Environmental Response Management Application (ERMA®), described below.
- Completing scientifically based field experiments and tests of response tools in US Arctic waters, if permits can be secured. If not, continue to conduct experiments in test tank facilities and partner with non-US entities in Norway and Canada to conduct field experiments in foreign waters.
- Identifying resource and infrastructure shortfalls for high-risk scenarios, and assessing strategies to address those shortfalls.
- Educating and involving stakeholders and the public on the various detection and mitigation techniques and baseline and subsistence issues.

RESPONSE EFFECTIVENESS

- Improving the performance of mechanical oil recovery systems in ice-infested water.
- Improving in situ burning techniques, which may minimize the volume of oil in the water.
- Quantifying the environmental effects of in situ burning, including smoke and residue products, so they may be included in the response assessment analysis, to assist in deciding the best approach for remediation as a function of in situ conditions.
- Improving the effectiveness of chemical herders that have been effective in scavenging oil from broken ice, expanding

the window of opportunity for recovery, and improving the cleanup process. Additional research may improve the performance of herders in Arctic conditions, characterized by ice, waves, and cold water.

- Evaluating dispersants in Arctic conditions. Dispersants were used extensively in the Deepwater Horizon oil spill cleanup. The effectiveness and toxicity of the dispersants, and their ability to disperse oil when injected at the source of submerged leaks, are topics of considerable research, but not under conditions that exist in polar regions.
- Evaluating the gaps in informational, logistical, communications, and infrastructure needs that currently exist in responding to spills, such as those described in the March 2008 report of the NOAA/UNH co-led Coastal Response Research Center (CRRC; http://www.crrc.unh.edu/workshops/arctic_spill_summit/arctic_summit_report_final.pdf).

- Undertaking research into the human dimension of spills. What are the impacts of Arctic spills on human beings? Factors to consider include the health and well-being of first responders and of local residents exposed directly and indirectly to petroleum products (such as through bio-accumulation and subsistence consumption of wildlife).
- Determining the effects of dispersed oil on the Arctic eco-systems, with assessments of the toxicity of dispersed oil and dispersants on benthic flora and fauna, and, in particular, marine mammals and sea birds.
- Analyzing the research and data needs for the Natural Resource Damage Assessment and Restoration Program (NRDA Restoration Program) process and for restoration projects.

Funding of Oil Spill Research

According to a recent report from the Government Accountability Office (GAO-11-319, March 2011), federal agencies that are members of ICCOPR have expended about $164M on oil pollution research from fiscal 2000 through 2010 (Table 1). Most of the funds ($145M) come from the Oil Spill Liability Trust Fund (OSLTF) authorized by the Oil Pollution Act of 1990 (OPA90). OSLTF is funded by a tax on petroleum production and importation, originally established at $0.05 per barrel, and later increased to $0.08 in 2008.

Beyond the trust funds, agencies have spent only an additional $18M on oil pollution research in over a decade, and only a fraction of that on spills in ice-covered waters, an area that ICCOPR has identified as an important need. Clearly, since the Deepwater Horizon incident, expenditures have increased, and the expenditures in 2011 and 2012 are likely higher than in recent years.

We note that NOAA is only federal agency with responsibilities for oil spill preparedness, response, and restoration, assigned by OPA90, which does not receive a direct appropriation from the OSLTF for research and development.

We further note that the manner in which research funds are expended by agencies varies widely. Some agencies, seeking expertise from beyond their own staff, issue calls for proposals and Broad Agency Announcements, and may also use a peer-review process to select projects for funding. Others follow a contractual approach, or expend the funds internally, within the agency.

With respect to the funding of the Oil Spill Recovery Institute (OSRI), created by OPA90, and described below, resources for oil spill research are tied to the interest earned on the *Exxon Valdez* oil spill settlement. Recently, funding for research has been approximately $1M per year.

Table 1. Federal agency funding for oil pollution research, both trust and agency funds, FY 2000–2010 in $M.

Agency	2000	2001	2002	2003	2004	2005	2006	2007	2008	2009	2010	Total
BOEMRE*	$7.1	$6.9	$6.8	$6.7	$7.5	$7.9	$7.5	$7.5	$7.1	$6.6	$6.2	$77.8
USCG	$4.7	$4.8	$4.8	$4.3	$4.1	$2.3	$2.8	$2.1	$2.1	$0.6	$0.7	$33.3
EPA	$1.1	$1.1	$1.1	$1.1	$1.0	$1.0	$0.9	$0.8	$0.9	$0.7	$0.6	$10.3
NASA	$0.0	$0.0	$0.0	$0.0	$0.0	$0.0	$0.0	$0.0	$0.4	$0.0	$0.0	$0.4
Navy	$4.3	$3.5	$1.2	$0.4	$0.3	$0.3	$0.2	$0.3	$0.6	$0.4	$0.6	$12.1
NOAA	$0.0	$0.0	$0.0	$0.0	$2.3	$2.2	$3.3	$3.2	$0.0	$0.0	$0.0	$11.0
PHMSA**	$0.0	$0.0	$0.0	$0.0	$3.4	$3.3	$2.1	$2.0	$3.4	$2.2	$2.2	$18.6
Annual Total	**$17.2**	**$16.3**	**$13.9**	**$12.5**	**$18.6**	**$17.0**	**$16.8**	**$15.9**	**$14.5**	**$10.5**	**$10.3**	**$163.5**

*BOEMRE was formerly MMS. Expenditures include about $3M/yr for the operation and maintenance of the Ohmsett facility.

** PHMSA is Pipeline and Hazardous Materials Safety Administration.

Data from the March 2011 GAO-11-319 report on federal oil and gas titled, *Interagency Committee Needs to Better Coordinate on Oil Pollution Prevention and Response*, http://www.gao.gov/assets/320/317056.pdf.

FEDERAL ARCTIC MARINE OIL SPILL RESEARCH EFFORTS

Department of the Interior

- Minerals Management Service (MMS)
- Bureau of Ocean Energy Management, Regulation and Enforcement (BOEMRE)
- Office of Natural Resources Revenue (ONRR)
- Bureau of Ocean Energy Management (BOEM)
- Bureau of Safety and Environmental Enforcement (BSEE)
- US Geological Survey (USGS)

MMS, BOEMRE, ONRR

Research programs funded by MMS, BOEMRE, BOEM, and BSEE are listed in an accompanying online table (http://www.arctic.gov/publications/oil_spills_tableA.pdf).

The Minerals Management Service (MMS) was created on January 19, 1982, nearly 30 years after Congress passed two milestone Acts—the Submerged Lands Act and the Outer Continental Shelf (OCS) Lands Act. This date was also 28 years after the first OCS lease sale was held. MMS was charged with resource management, safety, environmental protection, and revenue collection.

Most of the reports that analyzed the Deepwater Horizon disaster issued recommendations for industry and government, including changes in MMS structure and procedures. MMS had a broad mandate with inherently conflicting missions, and was under-resourced for the remarkable expansion of offshore drilling that took place over the last several decades.

On May 19, 2010, Department of Interior Secretary Salazar signed a Secretarial Order that separated MMS into three entities, the Bureau of Ocean Energy Management (BOEM), the Bureau of Safety and Environmental Enforcement (BSEE), and the Office of Natural Resources Revenue (ONRR). These entities oversee energy leasing, safety and environmental protection enforcement, and revenue collection, respectively. On June 21, 2010, MMS was renamed Bureau of Ocean Energy

Management, Regulation, and Enforcement (BOEMRE). To complete the reorganization, BOEMRE was replaced by BOEM and BSEE on October 1, 2011.

MMS/BOEMRE has historically leveraged research funds with industry and others to conduct research and development of oil spill technologies in Arctic waters. From 1997 through 2008, MMS/BOEMRE successfully developed, implemented, and conducted 31 projects directly related to Arctic oil spill response. More than 40% of these projects were jointly funded by state and federal government agencies, academia, private industry, and foreign governments.

The Oil Spill Response Research Program, described in the 2009 report *Arctic Oil Spill Response Research and Development Program: A Decade of Achievement* (http://www.iccopr.uscg.gov/iccopr/i/files/MMSArcticResearch_2009.pdf) focused on remote sensing and surveillance, mechanical response, chemical treating agents including dispersants, and in situ burning. This research included conducting operational research experiments with oil in small and large test tanks, at sea, and in ice to test many different types of oil spill response technologies and methodologies.

A review of this paper by the World Wildlife Fund, published in December 2009 and prepared with the assistance and technical expertise from Harvey Consulting, LLC, is titled, *Not So Fast: Some Progress in Spill Response, but US Still Ill-Prepared for Arctic Offshore Development*. It focuses on six findings regarding oil spill response in Arctic waters, and concludes, "…despite progress, significant gaps remain in the availability of effective oil spill response tools for the Arctic." WWF also called for "a response gap analysis in the Alaskan Arctic that would fully disclose and quantify the percentage of time during which local conditions exceed the demonstrated limits of spill response systems."

We note that the Canadian federal government has conducted such a response gap analysis for the Canadian Beaufort Sea and the Canadian Davis Strait. Canada's National Energy Board commissioned SL Ross Environmental Research for the work, and the report is available at https://www.neb-one.gc.ca/ll-eng/livelink.exe?func=ll&objId=702787&objAction=browse.

The Environmental Studies Program (http://www.boem.gov/Studies) has a broad remit to inform policy decisions on the development of the OCS by developing, conducting, and overseeing scientific research efforts. By region, Alaska receives significant attention, and research focuses on protected and endangered species, oceanography, biology, subsistence and traditional knowledge studies, and economic modeling. Other studies consider the fate and effects of oil in ice, and remote sensing and modeling of physical and biological systems. These programs have now been distributed between BOEM and BSEE, as described below.

BOEM

The Bureau of Ocean Energy Management (BOEM) manages the exploration and development of the nation's offshore resources. It seeks to appropriately balance economic development, energy independence, and environmental protection through oil and gas leases, renewable energy development, and environmental reviews and studies. BOEM is responsible for the Five Year OCS Oil and Gas Leasing Program that includes assessments, inventories, and production projections. BOEM administers oil and gas lease sales and offshore renewable energy programs, and conducts environmental reviews and studies. Of particular interest to this white paper are the Alaska Annual Study Plans and the Alaska Region Ongoing Studies that divide efforts into categories of Physical Oceanography, Fates and Effects, Habitat and Ecology,

Marine Mammals and Protected Species, Social Systems, Information Management, and Integrated Studies. The latest compilation of ongoing studies is on the BOEM website at http://www.boem.gov/uploadedFiles/BOEM/Environmental_Stewardship/Environmental_Studies/Alaska_Region/Alaska_Studies/Alaska_Ongoing_Studies.pdf.

In addition to current studies on Arctic biological communities (e.g., fish, sea birds, benthos, and marine mammals), the research program includes modeling of Arctic Ocean meteorology, circulation patterns, currents and their tracking by high-frequency radar, and the location and recurrence of polynyas (areas of open seawater surrounded by sea ice).

The University of Alaska Coastal Marine Institute (CMI) was created by a cooperative agreement between the University of Alaska and the US Department of the Interior Minerals Management Service Alaska Region to study coastal topics associated with the development of natural gas, oil, and minerals in Alaska's outer continental shelf. Many of the CMI-funded projects address issues related to fisheries, biomonitoring, physical oceanography, and the fate of oil. Research projects funded by the CMI are required to have at least one investigator from the University of Alaska. Cooperative research between University of Alaska scientists and various state agencies is also encouraged. Current research topics include movement and tracking of sea ice and polynyas, fish and benthic organism assessments, subsistence use, and effects of climate change. A full description of the CMI and their activities can be found at http://www.sfos.uaf.edu/cmi.

BSEE

The mission of the Bureau of Safety and Environmental Enforcement (BSEE) is to promote safety, protect the environment, and conserve resources offshore. To ensure that industry operations on the OCS incorporate the best available and safest technologies, BSEE attempts to enhance response technologies and capabilities through the Oil Spill Response Research (OSRR) Program. For more than 25 years, OSRR has funded a comprehensive and enduring research program to improve oil spill response technologies. The major focus of the program is to improve the knowledge and technologies used to detect, contain, and clean up oil spills on the

US OCS. Current OSRR projects cover a wide spectrum of oil spill response issues and include laboratory, mesoscale, and full-scale field experiments. Major topic areas, some of which are studied at Ohmsett, include remote sensing and detection, physical and chemical properties of crude oil, mechanical containment and recovery, chemical treating agents and dispersants, in situ burning, and deepwater operations.

The Ohmsett oil spill research facility, located in Leonardo, New Jersey, is operated and maintained by BSEE through a contract with MAR Inc. of Rockville, Maryland. The facility is the largest outdoor saltwater wave/tow tank facility in North America and is the only facility where full-scale oil spill response equipment testing, research, and training can be conducted in a marine environment with oil under controlled environmental conditions (waves and oil types). The tank's wave generator creates realistic sea environments, while state-of-the-art data collection and video systems record test results. The tank has been used to test oil spill containment/cleanup equipment and techniques, to test new designs in response equipment, to validate research findings, and to conduct training with actual oil spill response technologies. Partnering with CRREL, oil spills mitigation tests in ice-infested water (created using ice blocks) have been conducted at the Ohmsett facility. These tests include the Mechanical Oil Recovery in Ice-Infested Waters (MORICE) system and testing of dispersants in conjunction with a wave field. For more information see http://ohmsett.com/facility.html.

BSEE also operates the National Offshore Training Center with a curriculum that is designed to train new inspectors and to keep others up to date on emerging technologies and processes.

In December 2011, BSEE posted Broad Agency Announcement Number E12PS00012 for Proposed Research on Oil Spill Response Operations in the US Outer Continental Shelf. Two of the 10 topics in the BAA focused on ice and oil.

Additional helpful urls include:
- BSEE's website for oil spill response research: http://www.bsee.gov/Research-and-Training/Oil-Spill-Response-Research-(OSRR).aspx
- BSEE's Arctic oil spill response projects: http://www.bsee.gov/Research-and-Training/Technology-Assessment-and-Research/tarprojectcategories/Arctic-Oil-Spill-Response-Research.aspx
- BSEE's two most recent (FY12) projects: http://www.bsee.gov/Research-and-Training/Technology-Assessment-and-Research/Project1007.aspx and http://www.bsee.gov/Research-and-Training/Technology-Assessment-and-Research/Project1000.aspx

USGS

In order to pursue a comprehensive, science-based approach to energy development on the OCS, Department of Interior Secretary Salazar directed the US Geological Survey (USGS) to determine the gaps in scientific understanding of OCS energy development in the Arctic, particularly in the Chukchi and Beaufort Seas. That report was released on June 23, 2011, and is available at http://pubs.usgs.gov/circ/1370/pdf/circ1370.pdf. The report summarizes the large volume of existing scientific information, identifies where knowledge gaps exist, and provides initial guidance on new and continuing research that could improve decision-making.

Among the major areas noted in the report where additional scientific research, analysis, and synthesis could reduce uncertainties include the following:

- Developing a better understanding of the effects of climate change on physical, biological and social conditions as well as resource management strategies in the Arctic
- Developing foundational geospatial data on the Arctic Outer Continental Shelf

- Synthesizing existing scientific information on a wide range of topics on the Arctic
- Building upon advances in spill-risk evaluation and response knowledge by developing better information on key inputs to spill models (such as oceanographic, weather, and ecological data)

- Improving dialogue and using collaborative, comprehensive science planning, both domestically and internationally

A fact sheet on the Arctic study is available at http://pubs.usgs.gov/fs/2011/3048. The full report is available at http://pubs.usgs.gov/circ/1370.

Department of Commerce

• National Oceanic and Atmospheric Administration (NOAA)

The mission of the National Oceanic and Atmospheric Administration's Office of Response and Restoration (OR&R) is to prepare for, evaluate, and respond to threats to coastal environments, including oil and chemical spills, releases from hazardous waste sites, and marine debris. To address the increased potential for oil spills in the Arctic due to increased vessel traffic and oil exploration and development, NOAA OR&R has several initiatives currently underway. For further information see http://response.restoration.noaa.gov/oil-and-chemical-spills/oil-spills/activities-arctic.html.

- The Arctic Environmental Response Management Application (ERMA®) is a web-based GIS tool that assists both emergency responders and environmental resource managers in addressing incidents that may harm the environment. ERMA® integrates and synthesizes real-time and static data (information such as the extent and concentration of sea ice, locations of ports and pipelines, and vulnerable environmental resources) into a single interactive map, providing a quick visualization of the situation and improving communication and coordination among responders and environmental stakeholders. The Arctic ERMA® was developed and supported through a partnership between the NOAA Office of Ocean and Coastal Resource Management, the Oil Spill Recovery Institute, BSEE, and the University of New Hampshire. Further information can be found at: http://response.restoration.noaa.gov/maps-and-spatial-data/environmental-response-management-application-erma/arctic-erma.html.

- NOAA OR&R is the lead science adviser to the US Coast Guard during oil spill response operations in Alaska and it maintains a role on the Alaska Regional Response Team. OR&R's expertise spans oceanography, biology, chemistry, and geology, allowing the response team to estimate oil and chemical trajectories, analyze chemical hazards, and assess risks to coastal animals, habitats, and important areas to humans. This team is led by regional Scientific Support Coordinators. OR&R has also initiated the Arctic Joint Assessment Team and has assisted the Arctic Council, Canada, and Norway in developing Arctic spill response techniques and plans for spills in Arctic waters.

- Baseline ecosystem information is also being collected to properly identify environmental risks as well as to determine the current status and health of Arctic natural resources for NRDA Restoration Program purposes.

NOAA OR&R has also developed and funded a cooperative research partnership with the University of New Hampshire (UNH) to further oil spill research. The NOAA/UNH co-led Coastal Response Research Center (CRRC) was established in 2004. The CRRC has supported many research projects, workshops, and working groups on the subject of oil spill research and development, and has published a variety of reports. The Center for Spills in the Environment (CSE) is another center, also at UNH, that expands the scope of interaction and cooperation with the private sector, other government agencies and universities. Both the CRRC and the CSE are administered by, and located at, the UNH campus in Durham, New Hampshire.

The CRRC participated in the Selskapet for INdustriell og TEknisk Forskning ved norges tekniske hoegskole (SINTEF; the Foundation for Scientific and Industrial Research at the Norwegian Institute of Technology) Joint Industry Program "Oil in Ice" through research efforts associated with detection of dissolved polycyclic aromatic hydrocarbons (PAHs) from oil spills using passive samplers in cold water and ice cores; transport, fate, and potential exposure of oil in ice; oil movement in sea ice; and biodegradation of oil in Arctic first-year sea ice. Current studies being supported by the CRRC and NOAA are investigating the effectiveness, physical transport, chemistry, and biological effects of chemical dispersants, in particular, those used during the Deepwater Horizon incident. Other activities include conducting studies on the physical and chemical changes in heavy oil as well as holding

workshops on oil spill response issues. Workshops focusing solely on the Arctic include:

- Northwest Arctic Borough: An Oil Spill Workshop (May 22–23, 2012)
- Arctic ERMA® (April 5–6, 2011)
- NRDA in Arctic Waters: The Dialogue Begins (April 20–22, 2010)
- US Coast Guard Arctic Response (April 23, 2010)
- Opening the Arctic Seas: Envisioning Disasters and Framing Solutions (March 18–20, 2008)

A full description of CRRC and CSE activities can be found at http://www.crrc.unh.edu.

Department of Defense (DoD)

- US Army Corps of Engineers (USACE)
- US Navy (USN)

Because DoD mission priorities are currently focused on regions outside the Arctic, DoD is not providing any direct funds for research related to oil spills in ice-covered waters. DoD also acknowledges that, consistent with the current and projected level of DoD activity in the Arctic, it is most likely that an oil spill event will occur within the civilian sector. Under these circumstances, DoD will play a supporting role in responding to the spill, as it did for the Deepwater Horizon response. While not providing direct research support, DoD is making important contributions on other levels, including:

a. Maintaining access to facilities and expertise at the US Army Corps of Engineers' Cold Regions Research and Engineering Laboratory (CRREL) to conduct research on all aspects oil spills in ice-covered waters. CRREL is an international center of expertise on cold regions science and technology with cold rooms and refrigerated hydraulic facilities. Facilities used for oil and ice research include the Ice Engineering Facility (IEF), Geophysical Research Facility (GRF), and the Materiel Evaluation Facility (MEF). While CRREL does not directly fund these studies, their unique facilities, and in-house experts provide the capabilities to test equipment and techniques in near-field conditions. Staff at CRREL and Ohmsett have partnered on research projects to capitalize on the synergy of the researchers at DoD and DOI. Oil spill projects conducted at CRREL are summarized at http://www.crrel.usace.army.mil/innovations/oil_spill_research.

b. Scenario-driven exercises to evaluate DoD's level of readiness for Arctic operations, including communication protocols and logistic and equipment support. Knowledge and technology gaps are routinely identified during these exercises and reported, highlighting opportunities for future work for DoD and non-DoD entities alike. Recently, these exercises have included oil spill scenarios that are sufficiently severe to require a request of support from the DoD.

- US Navy Fleet Arctic Operations Game, US Naval War College, Newport, RI, September 13–16, 2011
- NORAD/USNORTHCOMM Arctic Collaborative Workshop, National Defense University, Washington, DC, March 13–15, 2012

c. The Emergency Ship Salvage Material (ESSM) System consists of facilities that provide salvage and pollution control (Oil Spill Response [OSR]) equipment and operators on an emergency basis. The worldwide ESSM facilities routinely provide mutual augmentation of personnel and equipment. One such facility is located on Joint Base Elmendorf Richardson (JBER). The ESSM OSR equipment is designed to be transportable and sustainable in the field. Although not specifically designed for Arctic use, the equipment has been modified for the Arctic environment but not for sea ice. Lake ice, in shore, and clear sea operations are all exercised annually. Systems located at JBER include two Vessel of Opportunity Skimming Systems, three 36-foot self-propelled belt skimming systems, boom, bladders, boats, inshore skimmers, support vans, and lightering systems.

Department of Homeland Security (DHS)

• US Coast Guard (USCG)

The United States Coast Guard operates the Research and Development Center (RDC), located in New London, Connecticut. This center is Coast Guard's only facility that conducts research, development, testing, and evaluation in support of their missions. The center evaluates the feasibility and affordability of mission execution solutions and provides operational and risk-management analysis for all stages of the acquisition process. When appropriate, the RDC collaborates with relevant professionals in the public and private sectors.

The Research, Development, Test, and Evaluation (RDT&E) Program conducts applied scientific research, development, testing, and evaluation of new technologies. The program pursues technologies that provide incremental improvements as well as those with the greatest potential to strategically transform the way the Coast Guard functions. As part of the program, the RDC is evaluating new technologies and techniques for cold weather oil recovery and is documenting performance gaps. A series of increasingly complex demonstrations have been started in the Great Lakes, and are also planned in Alaska. The RDC just completed the second oil-in-ice demonstration within Sector Sault Ste. Marie at St. Ignace, Michigan. The objective of this effort was to evaluate response capabilities in cold weather by leveraging Coast Guard and other local assets before conducting a more complex demonstration in Alaska. The demonstration scenario involved a fabricated leak from a pipeline in the open waters of the Mackinac Straits in northern Michigan. Tests were conducted using a helix skimmer in ice and also fire booms to separate out sections of the ice cover. Other R&D projects include sensors to detect submerged oil spills by multibeam sonar, a laser line scan system, fluorescent spectroscopy, and in situ mass spectrometers.

The USCG held a two-day workshop on "Leadership for the Arctic" in April 2012 to discuss science and research, maritime safety, maritime stewardship, legal issues, and governance. This meeting helped develop context for Arctic policy decisions as the USCG prepared for the planned Royal Dutch Shell exploration activities in the Beaufort and Chukchi Seas in the summer of 2012, via the exercise Arctic Shield 2012.

Another joint tabletop exercise was held by Shell Oil on May 24, 2012, to exercise their Chukchi Sea oil spill response plan. In addition to the USCG, participants included representatives from DOI, EPA, NOAA, and the State of Alaska.

Throughout the summer of 2012, USCG cutters and aircraft conducted exercises and training off Alaska to implement plans to mitigate potential impacts from a pollution incident. At the same time, scientists at the USCG's RDC were developing new ways to rapidly deploy and support response equipment at an incident scene. Demonstrations of equipment and tactics were held on the Great Lakes, and additional exercises are planned for the winter of 2013.

Other Federal Agencies

Other federal agencies, including the Environmental Protection Agency (EPA), the National Institute of Standards and Technology (NIST), the Department of Energy (DOE), the Department of Interior's Fish and Wildlife Services (FWS), and the National Aeronautics and Space Administration (NASA) conduct research on oil spills, but because their research is not specifically in association with ice-covered waters, they are not described in detail in this report.

The interagency "Committee on Marine Transportation Systems" has created a "US Arctic Marine Transportation Integrated Action Team" (http://www.cmts.gov/Activities/ActionTeams.aspx) led by USCG, the US Department of Transportation Maritime Administration (MARAD), and NOAA. It is focusing on issues related to marine transportation in the Arctic. While not focusing on basic research, the group has discussed issues associated with applied research.

COORDINATION OF FEDERAL R&D EFFORTS

Many entities are involved in the funding and conduct of oil spill research. With declining federal budgets, it is important to avoid duplication and effectively establish the means to coordinate activities and joint funding opportunities.

The Interagency Coordinating Committee on Oil Pollution Research (ICCOPR) was established under to Section 7001(a) of the Oil Pollution Act of 1990 (PL 101-380, also referred to as OPA90 in this report). Chartered as a 13-member interagency committee, its mission is to "coordinate a comprehensive program of oil pollution research, technology development, and demonstration among the federal agencies, in cooperation and coordination with industry, universities, research institutions, state governments, and other nations, as appropriate, and shall foster cost-effective research mechanisms, including the joint funding of the research."

One of the tools that the ICCOPR uses to communicate their activities is the ICCOPR Biennial Report to Congress. This biennial report, required by Section 7001(e) of the Oil Pollution Act of 1990, describes the activities carried out by the ICCOPR in the preceding two fiscal years as well as activities proposed to be carried out in the next two fiscal years. All of the ICCOPR biennial reports from 1992 to present day are available on the ICCOPR public website with the exception of the report from 1999–2000, which was not submitted due to the Federal Reports Elimination and Sunset Act of 1995.

In addition to producing biennial reports, ICCOPR also maintains an Oil Pollution Research and Technology Plan. Development of an Oil Pollution Research and Technology Plan is required by Section 7001(b) of the Oil Pollution Act of 1990. ICCOPR prepared the original Oil Pollution Research and Technology Plan to define the roles of each federal agency involved in oil spill research and development. The original plan was submitted to Congress in April 1992. The National Research Council's Committee on Oil Spill Research and Development, under the auspices of the Marine Board, reviewed this plan. Using input from the Marine Board, ICCOPR revised the plan in May 1993 to address spill prevention, human factors, and the field testing/demonstration of developed response technologies. The current version of the plan, still based on Marine Board recommendations, is dated April 1997. ICCOPR is updating the 1997 Oil Pollution Research and Technology Plan and expects to be finished in Fiscal Year 2013. Once completed, this plan will be available to provide oil pollution research guidance to government, industry, and academia.

The US Coast Guard chairs ICCOPR, and the current membership (now standing at 14 since the split of MMS/BOEMRE into BOEM and BSEE) includes:

- Department of Commerce—National Oceanic and Atmospheric Administration*
- Department of Commerce—National Institute of Standards and Technology
- Department of Energy
- Department of the Interior—US Fish & Wildlife Service
- Department of the Interior—Bureau of Safety and Environmental Enforcement*
- Department of the Interior—Bureau of Ocean Energy Management*
- Department of Transportation—Maritime Administration
- Department of Transportation—Pipelines and Hazardous Materials Safety Administration
- Department of Defense—US Army Corps of Engineers*
- Department of Defense—US Navy*
- Environmental Protection Agency
- National Aeronautics and Space Administration
- Department of Homeland Security—Federal Emergency Management Agency
- Department of Homeland Security—United States Coast Guard*

* Indicates active Arctic-focused R&D, related specifically to oil spills in ice-covered waters

ICCOPR has evolved significantly over the past 20 years. In the early 1990s, after the passage of OPA90, in response to the *Exxon Valdez* oil spill, ICCOPR was actively engaged in fulfilling its responsibilities. However, by the late 1990s and into the early 2000s, activity waned, as funding for oil spill research diminished. Under current USCG leadership, in response to positive encouragement and increased scrutiny after the Deepwater Horizon incident, ICCOPR has been rejuvenated. The members are meeting quarterly, and have updated their charter and membership. They have developed a comprehensive website, and they are focused on addressing their mission and meeting their obligations as defined in OPA90. USARC recognizes and applauds this significant improvement in interagency effort, as led by the USCG.

The website includes a summary of related R&D: http://www.iccopr.uscg.gov/apex/f?p=118:366:1376080403462271.

The website recently added a "High Latitudes" link, to provide some of the resources that the ICCOPR uses to help identify and support research issues related to cold weather response: http://www.iccopr.uscg.gov/apex/f?p=118:357:3718783452980200.

OTHER ARCTIC MARINE OIL SPILL R&D EFFORTS

Nonprofit Organizations

OIL SPILL RECOVERY INSTITUTE (OSRI)

Authorized by the United States Congress through the Oil Pollution Act of 1990, the purpose of the Prince William Sound (PWS) Oil Spill Recovery Institute (OSRI) (http://www.pws-osri.org) is to support research, education, and demonstration projects designed to respond to and understand the effects of oil spills in the Arctic and sub-Arctic marine environments. The OSRI 2011–2015 Research Plan (http://www.pws-osri.org/business/science_plan.pdf) provides detailed program goals and objectives in four major areas:

a. *Understand*. Attain an interdisciplinary understanding of the fate and effects of spilled oil in Arctic and sub-Arctic marine environments, and the recovery of those environments following a spill.
b. *Respond*. Enhance the ability of oil spill responders to mitigate impacts of spills in Arctic and sub-Arctic marine environments.
c. *Inform*. Disseminate information and educate the public on the issues of oil spill prevention, response, and impacts.
d. *Partner* (as per efforts associated with the Interagency Arctic Research Policy Committee).

The OSRI website provides a comprehensive list of all the projects that have been supported, by year and category of research. Recent projects of particular interest in the Arctic include:

1. Support for NOAA's Arctic Environmental Response Management Application (ERMA®) (see NOAA section for more on ERMA®)
2. Detection and mapping of oil spills under sea ice (DAMOS), Scottish Association for Maine Science, and Woods Hole Oceanographic Institution (2011 and 2012). This project, which includes tests at CRREL's Geophysical Research Facility, demonstrates that oil can be found under ice with existing technologies. Off-the-shelf instruments, including cameras and sonar systems, were mounted on an AUV or ROV.
3. Oil in Ice: Transport, Fate, and Potential Exposure, University of Alaska, Fairbanks (2009, 2008). This project was a portion of a larger project funded by the CRRC to examine the transport of various components of hydrocarbons through sea ice, to examine the biodegradation potential of those components, and to model the combined results.
4. Support for the National Academy of Sciences study, "Responding to Oil Spills in the Arctic Marine Environment."

Industry (US and Non-US)

ALASKA CLEAN SEAS (ACS)

ACS provides response services to the Alaska North Slope Crude Oil Producers and the first 167 miles of the Trans-Alaska Pipeline System. The company is a not-for-profit oil removal response organization that began operations in 1979. Today, ACS serves 10 member companies. ACS trains responders in Alaska and at Ohmsett and CRREL facilities and at the Prince William Sound Community College in Valdez, Alaska. ACS participates in research to improve equipment needed to respond to spills in the Arctic. Recent research efforts involved using ground-penetrating radar to detect oil under the ice and in developing a helicopter-based oil-under-ice detection system. Currently, ACS is in the design phase of an oil and ice-testing tank at Prudhoe Bay, Alaska, in partnership with CRREL. The design criteria include nonferrous construction to minimize electromagnetic interference for testing oil detection antennae and sufficient depth for testing ROV/AOV based systems.

JOINT INDUSTRY PROGRAMS (JIP)

For oil companies developing high-latitude natural resources, "stewardship" means investing in research to improve the oil spill response technologies and methods for use in the Arctic region. The oil companies' first priority must be prevention of oil spills. However, in the event of a spill, it is essential to have proven techniques and methodologies to reduce environmental damage. If an oil company uses company funds to develop a technique, the result is often proprietary, though results are sometimes presented at related conferences. Industry often supports Joint Industry Programs (JIPs), and depending on the nature of the program, the results may be presented publicly. JIPs are funding mechanisms for the oil industry and for government agencies (such as DOI) to leverage their research dollars to find a solution to a common problem.

Oil spill prevention remains a priority for the oil and gas industry and the ability to prevent and respond to oil spills is essential to achieve licence to operate. Substantive technological advances to detect, contain, and clean up spills in Arctic environments have been made by industry in the past decade. Uniting efforts and knowledge through a JIP increases opportunities to test equipment, conduct field experiments, develop oil spill response technologies and methodologies, and raise awareness of existing industry oil spill response capabilities in the Arctic region. Sharing knowledge, not only within the industry, but also with authorities, academic institutions, and nongovernmental institutions is crucial.

American Petroleum Institute and the Joint Industry Program on Oil Spill Recovery in Ice: *Spill Response in the Arctic Offshore*

Published in February 2012, this report (http://www.api.org/~/media/Files/EHS/Clean_Water/Oil_Spill_Prevention/Spill-Response-in-the-Arctic-Offshore.pdf) describes some of the challenges of responding to oil spills in the offshore Arctic, and discusses how industry has used results from research, technology development, and experimentation to respond to spills. The report was authored by consultants from SL Ross Environmental Research, DF Dickins Associates, and Polaris Applied Sciences, two of which are described below in the section "Private Consultants."

International Association of Oil & Gas Producers: Arctic Oil Spill Response Technology—Joint Industry Program

To build on existing research and improve the technologies and methodologies for Arctic spill response, the oil and gas industry established an Arctic Oil Spill Response Technology—Joint Industry Program (Arctic Oil Spill Response JIP) in January 2012, managed by the International Association of Oil & Gas Producers (OGP). The goal of this effort is to further improve oil spill response technologies through international research programs aimed at enhancing industry knowledge and capabilities in the areas of Arctic oil spill response. Nine oil companies are sponsoring the program: BP, Chevron, ConocoPhillips, Eni, ExxonMobil, North Caspian Oil Company, Shell, Statoil, and Total. Figure 1, provided as a personal communication from Joseph Mullin (Arctic JIP program manager), outlines the organization of the JIP. All results from the Arctic Oil Spill Response Technology JIP will be published and made publicly available. Research initiatives under this JIP include:

- *Fate of dispersed oil under ice.* Develop a numerical model capable of predicting the fate of a dispersed oil plume that develops under ice.
- *Dispersant testing under realistic conditions.* Define the operational limits of chemical dispersant and mineral fines in Arctic marine waters.
- *Environmental impacts of Arctic spills and Arctic spill response technologies.* Identify and conduct the research necessary to improve the knowledge base that supports NEBA (net environmental benefit analysis) and decision-making.

- *Trajectory modeling in ice.* Produce a verified/validated model that combines ice movement and spilled oil in ice to advance the state of knowledge of oil spill trajectory modeling in ice.
- *Oil spill detection and monitoring in low visibility and ice.* Identify and conduct the research necessary advance oil spill remote-sensing and mapping capabilities and technologies in darkness and low visibility, in broken ice, and under ice. Detect and track plumes that will develop if dispersants are used to control continuous subsea releases.
- *Mechanical recovery in ice.* Identify new approaches to facilitate the development of new or improved mechanical recovery equipment for use in the Arctic.
- *In situ burning state of knowledge.* Prepare materials to raise the awareness of industry, regulators and external stakeholders of the significant body of knowledge that currently exists on all aspects of in situ burning.
- *Aerial ignition systems.* Provide technology improvement that delivers a safe, reliable, and precise means of aerial ignition and improve oil slick targeting to support use of in situ burning.

- *Chemical herders to expand in situ burning window of opportunity.* Define the operational limits of chemical herders to allow in situ burning in open water and among broken ice.
- *Field research.* Evaluation of countermeasure technologies and conduct related research in a field setting.

The JIP projects, identified as "OSRT-JIP," are listed in an online table that accompanies this white paper (http://www.arctic.gov/publications/oil_spills_tableA.pdf). More information can be found at http://www.ogp.org.uk/news/press-releases/industry-programme-to-strengthen-arctic.

SINTEF: THE FOUNDATION FOR SCIENTIFIC AND INDUSTRIAL RESEARCH (NORWAY)

SINTEF is a broadly based, multidisciplinary research organization that partners with the Norwegian University of Science and Technology (NTNU) in Trondheim, and collaborates with the University of Oslo. SINTEF offers services based on their experience with modeling, testing of oils in their laboratories and large-scale facilities, and numerous, real-time oil spill studies and analyses. The SINTEF SeaLab is specifically designed for oil spill R&D and includes laboratories and mesoscale facilities for conducting experiments associated with development of underwater production of oil, as well as problems related to oil spills for ice-infested and coastal waters with complex current patterns. For more information see http://www.sintef.no/home/Materials-and-Chemistry/Marine-Environmental-Technology/Projects-and-News/SINTEF-SeaLab.

SINTEF was the lead on a Joint Industry Program on Oil in Ice with funding from Total, Statoil, ConocoPhillips, Shell, Chevron, and AGIP KCO. This JIP was established in 2006 and completed in 2009. It considered oil spill response techniques for Arctic waters and the fate and behavior of oil spills in ice and under cold-water conditions. Key findings of the Oil in Ice JIP include:

- The research program provided a valuable knowledge base to plan, implement, and further improve oil spill response in ice-covered waters.

- Each response tool evaluated during the program demonstrated some merit in responding to an oil spill an Arctic environment.
- The availability of all the response options was considered as being the key to a successful oil spill response operation in Arctic conditions.
- A systematic way to predict the operational time frame for various response options was identified, with implications for the efficiency of spill response.
- Large-scale field experiments supported results from a number of small- and medium-scale laboratory experiments.
- Laboratory and field experiments suggested that in situ burning and chemical dispersion may be appropriate response methods.
- The presence of cold water and ice can enhance response effectiveness by limiting the spread of oil and slowing the weathering process.
- The window of opportunity for in situ burning and dispersant operations in ice-covered waters can significantly increase compared to an open-water scenario under certain circumstances.
- New technologies for mechanical oil spill recovery and dispersant application that, when combined with a large set of test data, will improve response planning and response operations.

21

and Robert Perkins of the UAF's Institute of Northern Engineering. A Powerpoint presentation, summarizing the results, can be found online at http://www.newfields.com/dl/alaskaworkgroup/JIP Program 2009-2011/JIP Summary Updates and Presentations/UAF-NewFields-Toxicology and Biodegradation in Arctic1feb2011.pptx.

STATOIL (NORWAY)

Statoil completed a large research program in 2010 looking at the technologies for oil spill response in cold and icy conditions. Existing tools (e.g., chemical herders, fire resistant booms, remote-sensing systems) as well as newly developed technologies (e.g., mechanical oil recovery systems, dispersant application systems) were tested in different environmental scenarios. According to Statoil, the key findings from the program are: (1) all the response techniques could be used in responding to an oil spill in an Arctic environment, depending upon conditions; (2) the time window for use of in situ burning and the use of dispersants in ice-covered waters can increase significantly compared with an open water scenario because of the presence of cold water and ice (ice limits the spread of oil, slowing down the weathering process); and (3) having all response options available is considered to be the key to a successful oil spill response operation under Arctic conditions.

The full report on the Oil in Ice JIP can be found at http://www.sintef.no/project/JIP_Oil_In_Ice/Dokumenter/publications/JIP-rep-no-32-Summary-report.pdf.

BARROW/JIP (ALASKA)

From 2009–2011, four companies (Shell Exploration and Production Company, ExxonMobil Upstream Research Company, Statoil Petroleum ASA, and ConocoPhillips) teamed to study the "Toxicology and Biodegradation of Crude and Dispersed Oil in the Arctic Marine Environment." The effort was managed by Jack Word of NewFields

Canada

CENTRE FOR OFFSHORE OIL, GAS, AND ENERGY RESEARCH (COOGER) (CANADIAN FEDERAL AGENCY)

The Department of Fisheries and Oceans Canada (DFO) established the Centre for Offshore Oil, Gas, and Energy Research (COOGER) in 2002 to coordinate its nationwide research into the environmental and oceanographic impacts of offshore petroleum exploration, production, and transportation (see http://www.dfo-mpo.gc.ca/science/coe-cde/cooger-crpgee/index-eng.htm). COOGER's mandate was expanded in 2009 to include ocean renewable energy (i.e., energy conversion

from tide, wind, and waves) in response to emerging technological developments, so that Canada can meet its future energy needs in an environmentally responsible manner. By building on existing regional expertise and infrastructure to coordinate research at a national scale, COOGER addresses its departmental mandate and industry needs by providing scientific knowledge for use to ensure safe and environmentally sound management of offshore oil, gas, and renewable energy operations.

Based at the Bedford Institute of Oceanography in Dartmouth, Nova Scotia, COOGER maintains an extensive oil spill research program in partnership with national and international agencies, including the Canadian Coast Guard, US EPA, NOAA, BSEE, the Coastal Response Research Center (University of New Hampshire), Cedre (France), SINTEF, Akvaplan-niva (Norway), and others in the private sector through Joint Industry Program (JIP) agreements under auspices such as the International Association of Oil & Gas Producers. With the expansion of frontier oil and gas development offshore of Canada, a primary focus of COOGER's research is to understand the fate, behavior, and effects of oil spills, and to assess the efficacy of countermeasure technologies.

COOGER operates advanced chemistry and biology laboratories to conduct bench-scale research as well as to provide analytical support to oil spill response operations. The group maintains state-of-the-art instrumentation for petroleum hydrocarbon analysis that include Iatroscans, gas chromatography-flame ionization detectors (GC-FID), and GC-mass spectrometers (GC-MS), which enable fingerprinting for the identification of source oils and the tracking of physico-chemical and biological processes on oil spilled at sea and/or stranded within shoreline sediments.

COOGER has led experimental field trials involving the controlled release of oil within Canada, in addition to collaborating internationally with others in the United States, Norway, France, and the Netherlands. These studies have established operational guidelines pertaining to the application of bioremediation, phytoremediation, and natural attenuation strategies for the remediation of oil spill impacted sites. COOGER has also been involved in the development of standard techniques for the identification of operational endpoints based on habitat recovery for oil spill response operations.

A key aspect of COOGER's research is centered on its wave tank facility that was designed specifically for the evaluation of chemical dispersant effectiveness (under different wave energy regimes) and the potential biological effects associated with their application. Recent studies have also been focused on the interaction of oil spilled at sea with suspended particulate material (SPM) and the processes controlling oil-mineral aggregate (OMA) formation that promote both dispersion and biodegradation of oil spilled at sea. The aim of this research is to provide information for the support of decision making on the spill response option to be taken based on net environmental benefit analysis (NEBA).

COOGER has conducted a number of research studies pertaining to oil spills in the Arctic. They have included shoreline studies on the bioremediation (by nutrient addition and tilling) and surf-washing to remove residual oil stranded within supra- and intertidal sediments. Recent field studies have included a program in the Gulf of St. Lawrence in the presence of broken ice during the winter to evaluate the feasibility of enhanced OMA formation as a spill response strategy for use under Arctic conditions. Arctic field experiments are also being conducted to determine the capacity of natural bacteria to degrade oil and chemically dispersed oil.

COOGER's expertise was called upon by the US government in 2010 to assist with monitoring the use of chemical dispersant during the Deepwater Horizon spill. The Centre's Executive Director, Dr. Kenneth Lee, is an international expert in oil spill research and sits on a number distinguished committees including the US National Academy of Sciences/National Research Council Committees on the "Effects of the Deepwater Horizon Mississippi Canyon-252 Oil Spill on Ecosystem Services in the Gulf of Mexico" and "Responding to Oil Spills in Arctic Environments."

ENVIRONMENT CANADA (EC)

Environment Canada's (EC) mission is to protect the environment, conserve the country's natural heritage, and to provide weather and meteorological information to Canadians. The diverse organization collaborates with research partners on a variety of initiatives and participates in the Arctic Council. Agencies within EC that have conducted oil spill research include: Conservation and Protection Agency, Emergencies Engineering Division, Emergencies Science Division, and Western Office, Technology Development Branch.

In March 1978, EC began the Arctic and Marine Oil Spill Program (AMOP) to improve the knowledge base and technology for responding to Arctic and marine oil spills. The AMOP Technical Seminar on Environmental Contamination and Response is organized annually by the Emergencies Science and Technology Section (ESTS) and covers research and development on a variety of topics related to environmental emergencies caused by spilled hazardous materials. For more than 30 years, the Section has run a continuing national program of R&D on:

- Properties, behavior, detection, measurement, and effects of spilled hazardous materials
- Modeling and remote sensing of spilled hazardous materials
- Spill countermeasures: evaluation, effectiveness, effects, and environmental benefits of mechanical and chemical treating agents
- Shoreline impact and restoration, specifically development of the Shoreline Cleanup Assessment Technique (SCAT)

The 34th AMOP Technical Seminar was held October 4–6, 2011 in Banff, Alberta, with more than 100 papers and posters presented. The 35th technical seminar was held on June 5–7, 2012, in Vancouver, British Columbia. The program is available at http://www.ec.gc.ca/scitech/default.asp?lang=En&n=A0477462-1.

A unique feature of EC-supported R&D is that results are related to actual spill incidents, providing assistance to spill responders and conversely feedback to the researchers on the application of their work. R&D priorities are set and assessed by committees of representatives from all levels of government as well as international government agencies. Technology transfer is an important component of the program and the group provides operational guides, manuals, and training as well as some aspects of contingency planning.

Over the past decade, ECs budget for oil spill research has been lower, and the level of activity has been reduced. EC continues to maintain sophisticated laboratories for contaminant and sample analysis, but budget reductions have eliminated many other field programs and research activities.

UNIVERSITY OF MANITOBA SEA-ICE ENVIRONMENTAL RESEARCH FACILITY (SERF) (CANADA)

The Sea-Ice Environmental Research Facility (SERF) has a covered tank that relies on ambient temperature for sea ice growth. The existing tank is 60 feet long, 30 feet wide, and 8 feet deep, and is primarily used to grow sea ice under various controlled conditions, conduct mesocosm-scale studies to enhance the fundamental understanding of how sea ice forms and melts on polar oceans, and gain insight into the processes that regulate the exchange of energy and matter between the ocean and atmosphere. Detailed studies in collaboration with field measurements are being conducted to improve ability to predict the impact of the rapid sea ice loss on the marine ecosystem, on Arctic and global climates, on transport and biogeochemical cycles of greenhouse gases and contaminants, and on the human use of sea ice. A second tank for conducting oil and ice studies is planned. See http://home.cc.umanitoba.ca/~wangf/serf.

Private Consultants

Private consultants are providing support to oil companies and manufactures of oil spill response equipment. The results of their work are not typically in the public domain, unless the work is associated with a Joint Industry Program. As an example, two firms active in JIP efforts are DF Dickins Associates and SL Ross Environmental Research.

DF DICKINS ASSOCIATES LTD (USA)

Dickins specialties include engineering and environmental studies associated with offshore oil exploration and development, coastal mine sites, and marine transportation. More recently work has been in the area of remote sensing of oil spills under ice. See http://www.dfdickins.com.

SL ROSS ENVIRONMENTAL RESEARCH (CANADA)

SL Ross investigates a variety of oil spill countermeasures in the laboratory and field, including dispersant testing, in situ burning evaluations, testing of skimmers and booms, development of equipment for shoreline cleanup and disposal, sorbent testing and evaluation, and behavior of oil spills. SL Ross has a laboratory facility, which contains a 10 m long wind/wave tank. SL Ross also uses Ohmsett, the refrigerated facilities at CRREL, and a custom-built wave tank located on the North Slope of Alaska. SL Ross staff have also conducted several major field studies in the open ocean and in ice involving evaluations of dispersants, skimmers, booms, burning, and oil behavior. See http://www.slross.com.

Other Current Activities of Interest and Published R&D Plans

ARCTIC COUNCIL

On an international level, the Arctic Council Ministers, at their May 2011 meeting, created a task force to examine the possibility of bringing the Arctic States together to address oil spill preparedness and response. The United States initiated this proposal, and agreed to co-chair the Task Force with Norway and Russia. The impetus behind the US proposal was twofold:

- That the Arctic Council take the lead in ensuring that the Arctic States are well prepared for, and able to smoothly coordinate collective response to, possible oil spills in connection with increasing human activity in the region (e.g., offshore development, shipping, pipeline construction)
- That the lessons of the Deepwater Horizon event inform the Arctic States in order to improve international coordination for response

The Task Force decided to negotiate an instrument—legally binding—on oil spill preparedness and response based on the 1990 International Convention on Oil Pollution Preparedness Response and Cooperation (OPRC), administered by the International Maritime Organization (IMO), to which all eight Arctic States would be party. The instrument, which would be a regional multilateral agreement under the OPRC (Article 10), is likely to establish a cooperative framework similar to the Arctic Search and Rescue Agreement. The Task Force is likely to recommend to the Ministers whether and how best to pursue future work in this area, such as possible substantive annexes to the framework instrument that address technical aspects oil spill preparedness and response.

Norway hosted the first negotiating session in Oslo in October 2011, Russia hosted the second session in St. Petersburg in December 2011, and the United States hosted the third session in Anchorage in March 2012. A fourth session was hosted by Finland in June 2012.

At the time of publication of this white paper, the most recent development was the fifth meeting, in Reykjavik, Iceland, during the week of October 8, 2012, which involved delegates from the eight Arctic Council member states. The Task Force concluded negotiations on the instrument, with only minor technical issues left to resolve. It is expected that the agreement will be signed by the Ministers in May 2013.

At their May 2011 meeting, the Ministers also directed the Arctic Council working groups, led by the Emergency Preparedness, Prevention, and Response (EPPR) working group (http://eppr.arctic-council.org), to develop recommendations and best practices for oil spill prevention. This work is occurring in close consultation with the Task Force, and will be submitted, together with the instrument, to the May 2013 Ministerial meeting.

US NATIONAL RESEARCH COUNCIL

National Research Council (Ocean Studies Board, Polar Research Board, Marine Board) is currently coordinating a study titled "Responding to Oil Spills in Arctic Environments." According the Statement of Task, the NRC will assess the current state of the science regarding oil spill response and environmental assessment in the Arctic region (with a specific focus on the regions north of the Bering Strait), with emphasis on potential impacts in US waters. The study is currently supported by several entities, including USCG, NOAA, BOEM, BSEE, US Arctic Research Commission, American Petroleum Institute, the State of Alaska, and others. The committee has been formed, and the initial meeting of this group is scheduled for December 17, 2012, in Washington, DC. The target date to complete the report is 2014 (24 months after the initial committee meeting).

US CONGRESS

In January 2011, Senator Begich re-introduced two bills related to Arctic oil spills and research:

1. S.203 | A bill to direct the Administrator of NOAA to institute research into the special circumstances associated with oil spill prevention and response in Arctic waters, including assessment of impacts on Arctic marine mammals and other wildlife, marine debris research and removal, and risk assessment, and for other purposes. SPONSOR: Sen. Begich, Mark [AK] (introduced 1/26/2011). CO-SPONSORS: None. COMMITTEES: Senate Commerce, Science, and Transportation. LATEST MAJOR ACTION: 1/26/2011 Referred to Senate committee. STATUS: Read twice and referred to the Committee on Commerce, Science, and Transportation.

2. S.204 | A bill to amend the Oil Pollution Act of 1990 to permit funds in the Oil Spill Liability Trust to be used by NOAA, the USCG, and other federal agencies for certain research, prevention, and response capabilities with respect to discharges of oil, for environmental studies, and for grant programs to communities affected by oil spills on the Outer Continental Shelf, and to provide funding for such uses and for other purposes. SPONSOR:

Sen Begich, Mark [AK] (introduced 1/26/2011). CO-SPONSORS: None. COMMITTEES: Senate Finance. LATEST MAJOR ACTION: 1/26/2011 Referred to Senate committee. STATUS: Read twice and referred to the Committee on Finance.

STATE OF ALASKA: DEPARTMENT OF ENVIRONMENTAL CONSERVATION'S DIVISION OF SPILL PREVENTION AND RESPONSE

The State of Alaska has substantial experience with oil and gas development in the Arctic. Alaska has one of the largest Arctic oil fields and has conducted substantial offshore Arctic drilling, approximately 70 wells to date, with a great deal of experience in the use of offshore platforms in ice conditions. Four offshore production units are in operation in Alaska's Arctic. There are also 16 offshore platforms in ice-infested Cook Inlet waters, the first of which became operational in 1964. This Arctic and sub-Arctic experience has led to a sophisticated regulatory framework for oil spill prevention and response in ice-covered waters, and a robust preparedness and response program. The State of Alaska is equipped, and has a drill and exercise program. This state and industry experience offers a useful perspective from which to shape future recommendations for additional research in ice covered waters.

Based on GAO report 11-319, published in March 2011 (available at http://www.gao.gov/assets/320/317056.pdf), the State of Alaska has had a spill prevention and response program since the 1970s. As a result of judgments entered in the criminal cases for the *Exxon Valdez* oil spill, funds were provided to the State of Alaska to enhance the ability of the state and industry to respond to oil spills. Since 1989, a total of $2.5M has been provided to the Alaska Department of Environmental Conservation (DEC) for projects under this program. The funds have been used for research programs directed toward the prevention, containment, cleanup, and amelioration of oil spills in Alaska.

In cooperation with other stakeholders, DEC has supported over 30 research and development projects dealing with subjects such as cleanup technology, nonmechanical response techniques, the fate and effects of spilled oil, oil spill contingency planning and preparedness, spill response training, incident management systems, and spill prevention. Research supported by DEC has been conducted by Alaskan-based oil-spill response cooperatives, private consultants, universities, and other state and federal agencies. Details of the research can be found at http://dec.alaska.gov/spar/perp/r_d/research_list.htm.

UNIVERSITY OF ALASKA FAIRBANKS (UAF)

The University of Alaska Fairbanks (UAF) submitted a pre-proposal to NSF to establish a Science and Technology Center (STC) for Oil Spill Prevention and Preparedness in the Arctic. UAF was invited to provide a full Center proposal by Feb 3, 2012. The proposal was submitted, but it was not subsequently selected for support.

Regardless, the concept is worth describing. The STC is envisioned as a center-based approach, partnering UAF with CRRC and others, to perform the necessary research and development to prepare for potential spills in the Arctic, including understanding impacts to the ecosystem and developing techniques to mitigate spills should they occur. New techniques for detecting, tracking, and monitoring the movement and fate of oil will be required. In addition, basic research into the current ecosystem baseline and expected behavior of oil in the presence of ice will be required to advance knowledge of the arctic environment. The Center aims to: (1) identify knowledge gaps through stakeholders and subject experts, (2) sponsor fundamental research in science relevant to the Arctic environment, (3) sponsor applied research with joint funding from industry as well as state and federal agencies, (4) administer fellowships and grants related to education in Arctic science and technology, (5) transfer knowledge gained via workshops, meetings, literature, training, and electronic media, and (6) create feedback mechanisms to continuously identify knowledge gaps and evaluate efficacy of results.

RECENT WORKSHOP: OIL SPILL IN SEA ICE— PAST, PRESENT, AND FUTURE

A workshop was held by Istituto Geografico Polare "Silvio Zavatti" on September 20–23, 2011, in Fermo, Italy (http://www.oilspillsinseaice.net). Thirty-tree delegates representing 12 countries addressed the question: "How can we design an

effective, integrated system for dealing with every aspect of a potential accident in ice-covered waters which involves the release of oil?" A key outcome of the workshop was a "Fermo Statement," which has been submitted to the Arctic Council for consideration by the by the Arctic Task Force set up by the Council to examine protection of the Arctic against oil pollution (see above under "Arctic Council"). In 2013, the papers given at the workshop will be published in a proceedings volume and, after refereeing, in a special issue of the journal *Cold Regions Science and Technology*. The delegates at the workshop summarized their points into 12 themes:

1. How best to stop a blowout
2. How to model oil spread
3. Tracking oil spills
4. Problems with in situ burning
5. The role of dispersants
6. The physics of large-scale oil entrapment
7. The biological consequences of oil spills
8. The rapidity of environmental change
9. Data sharing and management
10. A rapid scientific response
11. Delivery of the oil to the ice underside
12. The natural background

USARC RECOMMENDATIONS

The United States Arctic Research Commission (USARC) has long supported the existence of basic and applied research programs to improve methods to prevent and respond to oil spills in the Arctic region, and to understand the fate and effects of oil released into the environment.

In 2004, USARC published *Advancing Oil Spill Response in Ice-Covered Waters* (http://www.arctic.gov/publications/oil_in_ice.html), which defined a program and identified research and development projects to improve the ability of responders to address accidental oil spills in fresh- or saltwater marine environments where ice is present. This response program included spills that occur on or beneath solid, stable ice extending out from shore, as well as spills in areas of drifting ice floes, and on ice-covered shorelines.

In 2010, USARC published a white paper titled *USARC Recommends Steps to Expanded US Funding for Arctic/Subarctic Oil Spill Research* (http://www.arctic.gov/publications/oil_spill_wp.html) that recommended ways to invigorate oil spill research in the United States. Several of those recommendations have been implemented, or are in the process of being implemented. For example, the Interagency Coordinating Committee on Ocean Pollution Research (ICCOPR) is currently updating its research and technology plan for the first time since 1997, and NOAA is now co-chairing ICCOPR. Second, government and industry funding has enabled greater research on the basic ecological structure of the marine environment in the Chukchi and Beaufort Seas. Funds have been provided by BOEM, a consortium of oil and gas companies, and the North Pacific Research Board.

This white paper updates the 2010 publication and offers the following recommendations to encourage those who are undertaking research to consider these areas for additional work. We do not prioritize these recommendations, and we also realize that, in some cases, these recommendations are presently being acted upon. We look forward to the implementation of recommendations, peer-reviewed publications that stem from work performed in these areas, and, most importantly, to the practical application of knowledge gained in real-world situations.

Spill Delineation and Mitigation, Including Containment and Countermeasures

- Develop spilled oil detection and mapping techniques that are independent of ice conditions, are rapidly deployable, and can be quickly interpreted in the field. Specific techniques that need enhancement are satellite and airborne sensors for cursory assessment, with refined delineation via airborne and underwater systems.
- Field test and train various techniques by the responders to assure familiarity with the process before it has to be deployed for a spill.
- Place greater emphasis on R&D for source control, and optimize Arctic vessel lightering, Arctic tank and pipeline evacuation methods, and Arctic well capping/containment.

- Develop a database that collects, analyzes, and then summarizes data from actual Arctic oil spills. These data would be used to ground truth the range of operating conditions and equipment/human factor limitations that have an actual effect on oil spill prevention planning and oil spill response improvements. To this end, BOEM has initiated a study entitled "Oil Spill Occurrence Estimators for Onshore Alaska North Slope Crude and Refined Oil Spills" and another called "Loss of Well Control Occurrence and Size Estimators for the Alaska OCS."

Oil Spill Response Technologies for Cleanup and Recovery of Oil......

- Improve performance of mechanical oil recovery systems deployed in ice-infested water (especially in spring broken ice and fall freeze-up conditions).
- Test in situ burning, which can be a viable option for minimizing the volume of oil. Chemical herders have been effective in scavenging the oil in broken ice, expanding the window of opportunity for recovery, and improving the cleanup process. Additional research is needed to improve the herder's performance in Arctic conditions including waves and cold water, and analyze their toxicity.
- Develop robots and ROV/AOV to assist in the cleanup process, which can be very useful during times when human response is not possible.

- Test methods to recover oil trapped under ice. Improve tools to measure and map oil spill thickness to identify areas of pooled oil that may be thick enough to collect or burn in situ.
- Evaluate dispersant efficacy and impacts in Arctic conditions. Dispersants were used extensively in the Deepwater Horizon cleanup, with considerable research done and still underway to assess their effectiveness and toxicity. The impacts of Arctic environmental conditions on the effectiveness of the dispersants should be assessed, including their ability to disperse oil by injecting at the source of submerged leaks and their potential impacts on the local wildlife and its consumers.

Data Management Tools Currently Being Developed, and the Fate of Oil and Its Effects on the Environment......

- Quantify the environmental effects of in situ burning, including the smoke and residue, so they can be included in the response assessment analysis, to assist in deciding the best approach for remediation as a function of in situ conditions.
- Define the effects of the dispersed oil on the Arctic ecosystems, with assessments of the toxicity of dispersed oil and dispersants on benthic flora and fauna, in particular, marine mammals and sea birds.

- Assess environmentally sensitive areas. Much of the Chukchi and Beaufort coasts have been identified as areas of heightened ecological significance. Much of the shoreline zones are shallow and composed of ice-rich permafrost soils. The impacts of both crude oil and dispersed oil deposition on these shorelines and the cleanup techniques available should be assessed. BOEM has some ongoing studies of such areas, but more are needed.
- Conduct additional research on the efficacy, and the human health, biological, and toxicological effects of chemical herders.

- Provide federal agencies with basic data, as well as summary reports, from industry research projects. USARC recommends data sharing as a cost-effective mechanism to increase federal response capacity.

- Analyze the "Response Gap" in areas that will soon be developed, to statistically quantify current response limitations. A "Response Gap" is the period of time when oil spill response is not possible because one or more limiting factors preventing an effective response (e.g., weather, sea ice, wave height, darkness, and extreme cold). Response Gap analyses have been performed in several areas experiencing or anticipating offshore oil and gas development, such as Davis Strait and Cook Inlet. They provide critical insight into needed planning efforts and identify the weakest link in the response chain that needs to be addressed.

- Test existing technologies in the specific ice conditions of concern (i.e., spring breakup, deteriorating spring ice, and fall freeze-up). Actual oil spill experiments and field trials are needed in the Beaufort and Chukchi Seas, employing local oil samples to improve tactics, improve response equipment and train personnel.

- Create a clear, concise description of human safety limitations (for response operations) to be included in oil spill response plans.

- Assess prior R&D projects to determine if they produced useful results. Were measurable advances in oil spill response techniques achieved, and in actual field response capabilities?

- Reveal, in agency budgets, the funding allocated for research on oil spills in ice-covered waters. This funding should increase, given the emphasis on the frontier prospects in the Arctic.

- Establish regulatory benchmarks and Best Available Technology (BAT) regulatory requirements for oil spills. These requirements would parallel those set for air pollution controls to incentivize greater private funding of R&D, which is currently lacking.

- Use research results to help create a BAT database for Arctic response equipment. If such a database existed, and was required for the Alaska Department of Environmental Conservation (ADEC) and BSEE, then permit applicants and regulators would install the BAT, or explain why it is not technically or economically feasible.

- Create an Arctic Subcommittee under ICCOPR that would focus on Arctic spill prevention, preparedness, and response, and base it in Alaska, in order to enable local stakeholders, oil spill cooperatives, industry, and the State of Alaska to consolidate knowledge and to seek consensus on Arctic research priorities.

- Fund NOAA for oil spill research and development from the Oil Spill Liability Trust Fund (OSLTF), in light of the fact that NOAA is the only federal agency with oil spill preparedness, response, and restoration responsibilities under OPA90 that does not receive a direct appropriation from the OSLTF.

- Increase either the amount of time that federal agencies are given to review permit requests, or the number of technical staff, given the breadth of oil spill R&D.

- Increase the use of peer review and greater transparency in publications. R&D results need to be reported accurately, including full disclosure on the scope of work, results, and what was concluded.

- Increase efforts to better communicate the state of knowledge, and the value, of oil spill research to the public and to the media.

Acknowledgments

The authors thank David Dickins (DF Dickins Associates Ltd.), Joe Mullen (Association of Oil & Gas Producers Oil Spill Response Technology Joint Industry Program), Scott Pegau (Prince William Sound Oil Spill Recovery Institute), Rod Doane and Ken Lee (Centre for Offshore Oil, Gas, and Energy Research), Kate Clark, Debbie Payton, David Westerholm, Brendan Bray, and Celeste Leroux (NOAA), Susan Harvey (Harvey Consulting), Marilyn Heiman (Pew), Lori Medley (BSEE), Kemp Skudin (Navy), Walter Johnson and Rodney Cluck (BOEM), Kurt Hansen (USCG), and Larry Dietrick (Department of Conservation, Alaska) for comments and suggestions. Additional thanks go to Stein Erik Sørstrøm (SINTEF) for permission to use the SINTEF photos.

USARC Commissioners

Fran Ulmer, Chair | Anchorage, AK

David Benton | Juneau, AK

Mary C. Pete | Bethel, AK

Charles Vörösmarty, PhD | New York, NY

Warren M. Zapol, MD | Cambridge, MA

USARC Staff

John Farrell, PhD | Executive Director

Cheryl Rosa, DVM, PhD | Deputy Director

Kathy Farrow | Communications Specialist